T

Little of

Leadership

by Ben Morton

© 2015 Ben Morton

First Published in Great Britain 2015 by
mPowr (Publishing) Limited

www.mpowrpublishing.com
www.theleadershipadvantage.co.uk

The moral right of the author has been asserted.

A catalogue record for this book is available from the
British Library

ISBN – 978-1-907282-50-8

Design by Martyn Pentecost
mPowr Publishing 'Clumpy™' Logo by e-nimation.com
Clumpy™ and the Clumpy™ Logo are trademarks of
mPowr Limited

Dear Amanda,

Thanks for your support!

Best regards,

Ben

To all those I've had the privilege to lead.

Thank you.

Introduction

Within this book you will discover a series of quotes and micro-tips to inspire you to become the best leader you can possibly be. Leadership is a great privilege and a great responsibility. We owe it to those that we lead to be the best that we can be for them, not for ourselves.

Sometimes I sit back and pinch myself. Over the last twenty years I have had the privilege of leading many teams in a wide range of environments and settings. They have all given me great experiences and powerful lessons in leadership and teamwork. I am hugely grateful for them all.

I don't think for one moment that my leadership journey is complete. I know that it is my insatiable desire to constantly improve, to constantly be better for those I lead, that has made me successful.

For most people, becoming a better leader isn't about making one or two big changes.

Being a better leader is a mindset. Building better teams and growing as a leader has become a way of life for me.

Though science and psychology can help us to be better leaders, being a great leader or building a great team is *not* rocket science. The path to leadership mastery and developing a high performing team is about doing the basics. It is about doing the basics consistently well—day in, day out.

The very best leaders are those that seek out mastery in all that they do. The best leaders are the ones that are always looking for the next marginal gain or 1 % improvement—for them and their team. This is what it means to be a great leader and this is what it takes to become a high performing team.

~~Read~~ Lead on...

"The leadership capability of any team or organisation directly shapes its culture, how innovative its products and services are and the experience its customers have. In fact, the leadership capability of your organisation is the last remaining sustainable, competitive advantage that you possess."

" We are entering an age where many people no longer come to work simply for the pay cheque. If we are to inspire and engage our people to come to work and give their best every day, then we must make leadership development a key strategic imperative. "

"In short, better leadership and management equals lower staff turnover, equals less time recruiting and getting new recruits up to speed. It creates more engaged staff who are willing and able to successfully take on more challenging projects."

> **"**There are essentially three parts to a Leader's role. Doing Things— Managing Things— Leading People.**"**

" Because most of us didn't set out to become leaders, and most organisations don't measure managers against how they lead their people, the leading-people element of our role often goes to the bottom of the to-do list and this is the management-leadership trap. **"**

"The managment-leadership trap is the single biggest challenge for leaders and managers and it is a mistake that so many people unwittingly make. The problem lies in the journey to management. Being promoted from a functional expert, somebody doing the doing, to a manager who now has responsibility for looking after a team of doers and not letting go.

"

" When the pressure is on or when we are stressed, most of us default to a natural prioritisation of our to-do list. Doing Things—Managing Things—Leading People. This is a prioritisation that is fundamentally backwards and broken. "

> "When the work pressure starts to build, when we're busy or stressed, investing the time in coaching our people can be one of the first things to fall by the wayside."

"Reverting to doing things is addictive as it allows us to focus on the things that brought us to our chosen profession in the first place. This shifts our focus from our problems, to activities that we enjoy and thus changes our state to a much more positive and productive one. But these are not the actions of successful leaders. "

"There are two main dangers here. The first is the addiction to the chemical high we get from a quick shot of dopamine—this can turn us into busy fools. The second is that we fail to delegate to our people and they become disengaged and demotivated."

" The current pace of technological and social change in the world today means that we need a new set of leadership skills and behaviours for the future. What got us here won't guarantee success in the next ten years. "

"By the year 2020 we will have five different generations working side by side in the workplace all with different aspirations, motivations and needs. To get the best from the diverse workforce of the future will require more time and a greater focus on leadership."

" Many of the tools and techniques that we use to manage our people today were born out of the Industrial Revolution. These were designed to maximise the productivity of people in factories and warehouses. Yet we continue to apply this outdated thinking to the modern workforce and wonder why they are not more engaged. "

" Many managers bemoan the fact that their people do not think for themselves. They become frustrated that their people come to them for the answers all of the time. Yet, the reality of this situation is often not that team members can't think for themselves; it is that you have taught them not to think for themselves. "

" To be a great leader you need to understand how to get the very best levels of performance from your people. To get the very best from your people, you need to know how best to support them; how to coach them. "

"Coaching is about helping your team to become more effective. It's about improving their performance and it's about solutions. All of this gives them freedom and autonomy in their role which ultimately leads to higher engagement. Isn't that what every leader or organisation really wants?"

" Coaching your people is one of the most effective things you can do as a leader to develop your people and grow your business. **"**

"Bringing the skills of a coach into your leadership style allows you to challenge and develop your team's skills. It enables them to achieve the best possible results and to function as self-sufficiently as possible.**"**

" To deny a person the opportunity to solve their own problem, fundamentally misses what it is to be human. Our higher-order ability to solve problems and think creatively is what separates us from every other species on the planet. "

" If you invest the time in coaching all of your team, you will be rewarded with greater engagement, loyalty, a hunger for improvement and much faster development. The fundamental truth of the matter is that time spent developing your people is always an investment, never a cost. "

"Servant Leadership begins with a natural desire to serve first. It is about putting the needs of others ahead of your own and making sacrifices for them. In focusing more on our team members and less on ourselves we are being of genuine service to them. In doing so we will become great leaders and coaches."

" Remember that as a coach, it is not your job to provide the answers. Your job is to help those that you are coaching find their own answers. Exactly the same is true with leadership. As a leader you do not need to have all of the answers. "

"The sooner you accept that, as a leader, you do not need to have all of the answers and can let go of your need to appear invulnerable, the sooner you will unlock your true leadership potential."

"Success as a leader isn't about having all the right answers. It's about having the humility to ask the right questions.

In striving to become a great leader who utilises the skills of a coach, you are making a commitment to invest in and support your people all of the time—not just when you have time.**"**

"Great leaders and coaches build people's confidence and ability to act. They enable them to identify their own solutions. The real learning happens when you help the team member to surface their own answers and this is when lasting changes are created."

" The very best coaches, the truly world-class coaches, put all of their energy into helping the person being coached to become great. They focus fully on their team member and put all of their effort into listening to what they are saying—which creates a virtuous circle of high performance. "

"At its best, performance is about identifying what's working well so that you can replicate it over and over again. Whilst we know this to be true we often spend time reviewing the things that have gone wrong and fail to reflect upon and learn from that things that went well."

" Professional sports coaches work with hugely talented individuals and focus on moving their performance from good to great or from great to world class. The same is true of great leaders. **"**

"When the majority of us are learning a new skill our hunger for learning gradually decreases with the passage of time. Ultimately, when you have a team member whose hunger for learning or development has plateaued you need to find a way to re-energise or excite them. This is why we must give equal time to all in our team, not just the under-performers."

"Moods, energy levels and states are incredibly contagious and will spread through teams at an alarming rate given the chance. In this respect a frustrated high-potential can be just as damaging to your team as a demotivated underperformer."

"The ability to share detailed feedback in a productive, non-threatening manner is a critically important skill for leaders, managers and coaches. Ken Blanchard says that it is a sad reality that many people's gauge of whether they've done a good job or not is whether they have been shouted at by their boss recently."

" Feedback to a team member can be tremendously valuable, especially in helping to raise the team member's awareness of a potential blind spot. But useful feedback requires accurate descriptions of observed behaviours and the effects. "

" By committing to giving more feedback, the very thing that makes us feel uncomfortable, we are able to expand our comfort zone. It will not instantly make giving feedback the most comfortable thing in the world (although it may for some), but over time, by consistently doing it we are able to expand our comfort zone. "

"One of the key skills of a great coach is to remain impartial, not making judgments about your team member, their situation or actions. You may have tackled a similar challenge in the past yourself, but that does not mean your way was the best way. "

"As a manager-coach it's important to resist the temptation to switch into tell mode and assume that the way you tackled a situation, is the best way or the only way. By highlighting the challenges, sharing some of your experiences, and continuing to coach you can achieve some amazing results."

"

By bringing the skills of a coach into your day-to-day leadership style, you have the chance to profoundly grow and develop as a leader. If you fully commit to coaching then you will be transforming yourself from a command-and-control manager into a supportive and inspirational leader, enabling and inspiring others to act.

"

" As a leader or manager-coach you absolutely must approach your sessions with a great deal of clarity and integrity. It is not uncommon for manager-coaches to find that their interests and those of their team members are in conflict. "

"Be totally clear about your personal values, what you stand for. This is your foundation as a leader. When you are faced with difficult decisions or conflicting priorities your values will guide your decisions. They are your moral compass."

"For the expert manager-coach this is about moving seamlessly between coaching and mentoring. It is about flexing your style and utilising the skills as both a coach and mentor.**"**

> **"** Whilst the GROW model provides a framework and set of steps to follow, you should not allow it to drive the coaching conversation. The model is a tool to enable great conversations, not a process to be rigidly adhered to. **"**

" Consider using the GROW model to be like holding a butterfly in your hands. Hold onto it too tightly and you will crush it. Hold it too loosely and the butterfly will fly away. If you use the GROW model too rigidly you will kill the conversation. If you have no structure the conversation will be directionless. "

"Whilst your focus as a Master Coach is still firmly on respecting your team member's map of the world—and not suggesting or leading them down any particular route—you can help them to commit more fully."

" How can we ask our team members to focus on (and reflect upon) their performance if we do not do this ourselves? This isn't a sign of weakness; it is a sign of great strength that gives so many positive messages. **"**

"Many leaders and managers say that they have so much work to do that they do not have time to lead or put into practice the concepts contained in this little book. To make this statement is to fundamentally misunderstand what it means to be a leader. Leading is your work."

" The first step when getting off the busy-ness treadmill is to understand where you currently invest your time and then look to redress the balance. In doing this you take back time and control; this enables you to think, lead and coach your people to the best of your ability. **"**

" If we want people to follow us with blood, sweat and tears then they have to know who we are and what we stand for as a leader. The first step as a leader is therefore to get really clear on why we are leaders, the type of leader we want to be and what our core values are. "

" The best leaders
have the ability to align
people to a vision whilst
motivating them to
work passionately and
relentlessly towards its
fulfilment. **"**

"Everybody that we lead is somebody's son or daughter, husband, wife or partner. They are somebody's father, mother, brother or sister—in short, everybody that we lead is a human being who is the most important person in somebody's life. It is for this reason that to lead anybody is a great privilege and a great responsibility. This is why we must take our role as leaders seriously—we owe it to those that we lead and their families."

Ben Morton is an accomplished team-development consultant and leadership coach. His wealth of leadership experience and expertise means he is a highly sought-after, trusted advisor in all sectors from larger SMEs to global brands. Ben's corporate insight is enhanced by his military background, giving him a unique insight into the dynamics of successful teams and inspirational leadership.

Also avilable by mPowr Publishing:

Mission: Leadership—Lifting the Mask
by Ben Morton
978-1-907282-71-3

978-1-907282-72-0 (iBook Edition)
978-1-907282-73-7 (eBook Edition)

Don't Just Manage—Coach!
by Ben Morton
978-1-907282-60-7

978-1-907282-64-5 (iBook Edition)
978-1-907282-65-2 (eBook Edition)

Legacy—You Get One Life... Make it Remarkable
by Martyn Pentecost
978-1-907282-48-5

The Right Brain for Business
by Martyn Pentecost
978-1-907282-30-0

Lightning Source UK Ltd.
Milton Keynes UK
UKOW07f0315270216

269215UK00007B/14/P